COMING OUT AS AMBER

Sissification Stories

Jane Doe

CONTENTS

CHAPTER 1

My mother yelled from the main level of our house as I laid in bed in my room on the second floor. "David, are you almost ready? We need to leave!" I laid still with the covers pulled over my head as well as the rest of my body. Footsteps echoed throughout the home as my mom walked up the wooden staircase from the foyer to the upstairs hall where my room was the first on the left. I heard the doorknob turn before my mom peeked through the doorway.

I laid motionless as she stepped into my room and approached my bed.

"David, are you still sleeping?" She asked.

"What…" I said in a groggy voice. I pulled the blanket down to my neck before responding. "What time is it?"

"We're leaving for Grandpa's in ten minutes. Are you feeling ok?"

"I don't know…not really…my stomach started hurting last night, and I woke up with the chills."

My mother stepped closer to me and put her hand on my forehead. "You do feel warm." She said, sounding concerned.

"I heard Steven from basketball came down with the flu, I hope I didn't get it too." I said with drowsiness in my voice. "I can still probably go…I'll try to get ready…"

"You are not seeing my 89-year-old father if there's a chance you have the flu. Just lay down and we'll figure something out."

My mom walked out of the room and gently closed the door behind her. I could hear her walk back downstairs and make her way to the kitchen before informing the rest of my family of my illness. Their voices echoed through the tile floored kitchen up to my room.

"What! That's so not fair. Why does he get to stay home?" My younger sister, Gloria, complained.

"We're not going to take a chance with your grandpa. The flu could literally kill him at this point." My dad snapped back.

"Well, who's going to stay home and take care of him?" My mom asked.

"He's twenty-two years old. He doesn't need a babysitter." My dad asserted.

With concern in her voice, my mother asked, "But what if he needs soup or something to drink?"

"Then he'll get it himself. He's going to be fine." My dad stated.

"I can stay with him." Gloria offered.

"No, you're going to your grandpa's birthday party and that's final!" My dad yelled.

"Oh my god I can't believe I'm going to be stuck with you guys all weekend and David gets to stay home. This is so not fair." Gloria complained.

Sounding frustrated, my dad responded, "That's life honey."

I could hear the door to the garage open and luggage being hauled out to the car. After several minutes, a few sets of footsteps made their way upstairs to my room. The door opened to reveal my mom, dad, and sister standing in the doorway.

"We have to get going now. How do you feel?" My dad asked.

"Ok I guess. I just feel kind of weak and lightheaded. And my stomach doesn't feel very good." I responded with my eyes half closed.

"He is such a liar..." Gloria asserted, "he just doesn't wanna go."

"We have plenty of soup downstairs and I brought you a couple of water bottles." My mom said while ignoring my sister. My mom walked over and set the water on my desk beside my bed before leaning over and feeling my forehead again.

"Just rest up and call us if you need anything. We'll only be a few hours away if we need to rush home." My mom said.

"We're only going to be gone for the night. I'm sure he'll be fine resting until tomorrow afternoon." My dad said.

"Thank you." I said, after swallowing the saliva in my mouth. "I'm just going to try to sleep."

"We'll let you rest. I love you, sweetie." My mom said after giving me a kiss on the forehead. She walked over to my dad and stood in the doorway as he said his goodbye.

"Take care of yourself and get some rest."

"Have fun." My sister said sarcastically.

My mother gripped my sister's arm as they stepped out of my room and closed the door. I could hear them make their way down the stairs before walking through the kitchen and exiting into the garage. The sound of the garage door opening was followed by the car starting and pulling out. After hearing the garage door close, I popped up in bed and looked out my window that faced the street. As soon as my parent's car was out of sight, I threw the blankets off of me and jumped out of bed.

CHAPTER 2

I didn't enjoy lying to my family about being sick, but I disliked seeing my mom's side of the family even more. After my grandma passed, it felt like my grandpa had started to decay rapidly. His racist rants had become more unhinged as he spoke his mind without any sort of filter. It felt like he realized how little time he had left and was trying his hardest to pass down his knowledge while he had the chance. The only problem was that I found his 'knowledge' to be unsettling.

Being that it was his birthday, I knew that he would take every opportunity to grab the room's attention and tell one of his stories about the 'good ol days in the county'. Everyone would smile and nod along as he rambled on endlessly without any sort of coherent message. I couldn't sit through that again, so I decided to enjoy the day by myself.

After strolling downstairs to the kitchen, I helped myself to a bowl of cereal for breakfast. Pulling out my phone, I scrolled through social media as I munched on my food. Once I was finished, I made my way back to my room and opened up my closet.

Digging behind my shirts that were hanging up, I pulled out my travel worn suitcase and wheeled it out. After setting it on my bed, I unzipped the bag and opened it. My eyes lit up at the sight of my treasure trove of clothes, shoes, and makeup. I began pulling out the contents and laying them across my bed.

Avoiding my racist relatives was enough of a reason to pretend to be sick, but having an entire day to crossdress as I pleased was what I wanted more than anything. Because of the background of my parents and their families, I had to keep my crossdressing habits a secret and find opportunities to do it when they weren't around. After getting my degree in business, I was hoping to make enough to get my own place and have some space to explore my interests. Unfortunately, with my student loans and a job market that didn't pay very well for someone like me who was just starting out, I realized quickly that I would have to live at home until I could establish myself. Now that I finally had the house to myself for the entire day, I wanted to soak up every minute of it as my alter ego.

I quickly undressed and threw my pajamas in the laundry bin before looking over my outfit choices. As I brought my hand up to my face while trying to decide what to wear, I could feel some light stubble. I knew that in order to enjoy the day ahead of me, I would need to shave.

To keep my family from getting suspicious of my crossdressing, I used hair removal cream and shaved my legs, arms, and face often. Because my hair was kept short to nonexistent around my body, no one would blink when the little bit I had disappeared again. Although my body was almost completely hairless, the hair on top of my head was another story.

When I discovered my love for crossdressing a few years earlier, I had decided to grow out my hair and keep the length just past my shoulders. My sister liked to tease me about it, but most girls would compliment my long, thick, straight hair. After a few years of maintaining my hairstyle, it became natural to everyone around me.

Before stepping into the shower to shave, I brought my makeup and underwear into the bathroom and laid it out. I stepped under the shower nozzle and took a few moments to enjoy the warmth from the water flowing over me. Once I was ready, I continued by shaving the hair off of my legs and up to my waist. My chest and back had never grown any hair, except for a small patch around my belly button that connected to my pubic hair, so I focused on the little bit of hair that was present.

After spending thirty minutes making sure that I was smooth and soft, I turned the water off and stepped out of the shower. Feeling impatient, I quickly dried myself and slid a pair of red lace panties up my legs. The soft feel of the material against my skin was exhilarating. Having just a few opportunities to wear the panties since I bought them online, I still felt a rush every time I put them on. I put on my matching red push-up bra next and struggled to fasten it behind my back.

Standing in front of the mirror in the bathroom, I began pulling out my makeup from the small purse that I kept it inside of. Before putting on my face, I used another towel to dry my hair and tie it in a high ponytail. With my hair out of the way, I began by spreading foundation around my face.

I had spent many hours watching videos and tutorials online on makeup application, but unfortunately, I still felt like a novice. By the time I was finished spreading the foundation, I looked like a geisha. Feeling unhappy with how I looked, I cleaned it off and tried again. Using a much lighter coat of foundation, I tried to go with an everyday look. Surprisingly, on the third try, I was satisfied with the way it looked.

I continued by using some setting powder and applying it around my face and neck. Using some blush on my cheeks next, I swirled a light coat up high on my cheekbones. Trying not to go overboard, I kept it light and made sure that it looked natural.

As I moved on to my eyes, I began to get nervous. This was always the part I found the most difficult. I took a deep breath and told myself to just keep it light. I did my best to draw a thin black line on the eyelids and give a small wing at the end, like I saw other girls do. After nailing the right eye, I became far too eager and rushed through the left one. To my dismay, my eyelid stuck to the eyeliner pencil and skipped a few sections. As I went over my eyelid again, it felt like it became much thicker than the right eye. I grunted before cleaning it off and trying again.

Going much slower this time, I drew a thin line over my left eyelid and remained patient as I worked. Finally, having both of my eyes done with eyeliner, I used some light brown eye shadow to fill in the rest of my eyelids. To finish my eyes, I applied a healthy amount of mascara to my eyes lashes. Once they were to my satisfaction, I put my eye makeup away and pulled out my lipstick.

Moving ever so slowly and carefully, I outlined my cupid's bow first before filling in the rest of my lips. With my apple red lipstick applied, I pursed my lips and let my hair down. Grabbing a brush, I worked out the knots and made sure that my hair fell straight. My hair had a small natural curl at the end, which I had come to love while dressed up.

Once my hair fell how I liked it, I looked over my appearance in the mirror. With my makeup and hair to my satisfaction, there was only one thing left to do. It was time to slide into my high heels and dress for the day.

CHAPTER 3

After walking back to my room, I grabbed my favorite pair of red high heel pumps off of the bed. With a pointed toe and an ankle strap, I absolutely loved sliding the four and a half inch high heels onto my feet. Butterflies fluttered in my stomach as I stepped into the left shoe first and fastened the strap around my ankle. Once my right shoe was on, I looked down and squealed with excitement.

Taking a few steps back and forth across my room, I practiced my strut and struck a few poses. I hadn't felt so giddy since the last time I had the opportunity to crossdress. After getting my excitement out, I pulled out my red tea length dress that matched my high heels and carefully stepped into it. It was short-sleeved, with a zipper running all the way up to the base of my neck. With some struggling, I managed to pull the zipper all the way up behind me.

I felt a mix of nervousness and excitement as I twirled in my dress. It could've been years of sexual repression or the family ideals my parents tried to instill in me, but something about crossdressing always made me feel slightly guilty. Even though I didn't steal the clothes and wasn't wearing anything that belonged to my sister, I couldn't shake the feelings that would find a way to creep up. After hanging my head for a moment, I took a deep breath and put a smile back on my face before strolling downstairs.

Hearing my high heels click across the tile floor helped bring out my feelings of femininity. Although it was a simple act of just walking through my house, being reminded of what I was wearing by the sounds it made was delightful. I stepped into the kitchen and gave a twirl before walking to the front door. Taking a peek outside, I could see the empty street and trees across from our house.

Although we didn't have neighbors across the street, there were two on each side. Each house on our street was set back in the trees and had enough space between them so that you could not see the neighboring homes through the greenery. As I looked through the window next to the door, my heart sank.

A red car pulled into the driveway and parked just in front of the garage before its engine shut off. I crept back from the door and scampered up the stairs to my room. As I peeked out of my bedroom window that overlooked the driveway and street, I could see the car's door open.

From the short blonde hair and thin body frame, I recognized the visitor as my sister's best friend, Emily.

"What the hell is she doing here?" I said to myself out loud.

I stood frozen as she walked up to the garage and entered the code on the keypad. I felt paralyzed as I heard the garage door opening and Emily walking inside.

With the clothes I was wearing, a face full of makeup, and my hair styled, there was no way I could let her see me. I closed my door gently and locked it as I heard Emily walk into the kitchen. I took a few small steps backwards as she walked up the stairs and stopped at my door.

After hearing the handle shake, Emily called out through the door.

"David, are you in there?" She asked.

Hoping that she would think I was asleep, I stayed silent.

"David, are you ok? Your parents said you were really sick and I couldn't leave until I made sure you're alright." Emily informed.

Taking a few long, deep breaths, I saw a glimmer of hope that there may still be a way out of this.

"Uh, yeah." I responded in a low, breathy voice.

"Can you open the door? I brought something for you." Emily informed me.

"I'm feeling too achy to get up. Just leave it there, I'll...I'll get it later." I responded.

"Your parents said you have a fever and need to get some fluids in you. Why is this even locked when you're home alone, anyway?" Emily asked.

"I don't know. It must have happened by accident." I said, feeling agitated that she wouldn't leave me alone.

"How do you accidentally lock a door? What are you doing in there?"

"I'm laying down...I'm fine...you can just go...I'll be ok." I said while stuttering my way through my words. I felt cornered.

"Emily?" I called out after not hearing a response. "Emily? Did you leave?"

I stood perfectly still in my room as I tried to listen for Emily on the other side of my door. With each passing second, my heart pounded harder through my chest.

As I took one small step toward the door, the lock on the handle turned. Putting my hands out and rushing toward the door, I yelled "NO" just as Emily peeked her head into my room. Her eyes went wide before she braced herself against the door and prevented me from shutting it. I struggled against her for a few moments, but once she acknowledged what I was wearing, I knew it was no use to try to hide anymore.

"David, are you wearing a dress?" Emily asked as I leaned my back against the door with her on the other side.

"Were those your high heels? And whose makeup did you use?"

I ignored her questions and continued pushing against the door.

"Would you just stop so we can talk?! Why are you dressed in your sister's clothes?" Emily asked.

"I didn't touch any of her stuff!" I yelled.

"Then whose is it? If you don't come out and talk to me, I'm going to have to call your sister." Emily warned.

I remained speechless as I held my weight against the door.

"Fine, have it your way." Emily said while stepping back. The door slammed shut as I fell backward into it.

As I thought about the ramifications of a phone call to my sister, I clenched my teeth and swung the door open. A gleaming

smile appeared on Emily's face as she scanned from me from head to heels.
"Damn girl, you look fine." Emily said with a giggle.

CHAPTER 4

I hung my head in shame as Emily giggled in front of me. Until then, I had been careful to keep my crossdressing a secret. No one had ever seen me when I dressed up or acted girly. I was content to keep this a secret forever, but that was over now. As I heard a click come from Emily's phone, I looked up to see her taking a picture of me.

"What the hell are you doing?!" I screamed while lunging toward her. Emily scurried away and ran down the stairs. Forgetting that I was wearing high heels, I tripped and fell in the upstairs hallway while Emily ran down to the main level. I slipped my shoes off and stood at the top of the stairs while staring at her.

"Delete that." I said sternly.

"Not until you tell me what you're doing." Emily responded.

"What does it look like?" I yelled back while throwing my hands in the air.

"It looks like you faked being sick so that you could pretend to be a girly girl while your parents are away." Emily responded.

"So…" I said while shaking my head.

"So that's like, really big news. Does Gloria know?" Emily asked.

"Obviously not."

"Well, obviously your parents don't know either. Have you told anyone?"

"No! No one is supposed to know…" I paused as tears began forming in my eyes, "This wasn't supposed to happen."

I hung my head and walked back toward my room. After picking up my heels, I sat on my bed and began whimpering.

Emily walked up the stairs and stood at the entrance of my room a few moments later.

"Look, I'm sorry for being a jerk and taking a picture. I'll delete it right now." Emily said while opening up her phone. I watched as she pulled up the photo and pressed the delete icon.

"See, deleted." Emily said.

"Thank you." I said softly.

"I won't say anything to your parents but, this is way too big of a secret to keep from Gloria. She didn't know about you dressing up like a girl, but she knew you weren't sick. I'm pretty sure it was her idea to have me come over."

"Oh my god, just please don't tell her." I pleaded.

"I won't…but you should." Emily said.

"What? Are you crazy? She's just going to laugh at me and then tell everyone."

"I can help if you want. I know siblings can fight like crazy, but you know you can trust her when it's something serious like this."

I took a deep breath before responding. "I'll think about it…Thank you for being so nice about this."

"Don't worry about it. I know you'll pay me back eventually." Emily said while nudging my shoulder.

"Uh, how?" I asked.

"Well, maybe I can borrow your clothes instead of your sister's." Emily giggled.

After my talk with Emily, I felt a huge weight lifted from me. I was still nervous about what came next, but I knew that I had an ally that I could count on. I wiped off the makeup that ran down my cheeks and stood up from the foot of my bed. Emily gave me a big bear hug before offering to help clean up my makeup.

I showed Emily my makeup collection in my suitcase and sat at the foot of the bed next to her.

"This is all yours?" Emily asked while looking surprised.

"Yeah…" I said softly.

"How have you been keeping this a secret?"

"I usually just order stuff online and make sure I'll be home right when it arrives. And no one ever goes through my closet, so it was kind of easy honestly." I responded.

Emily wiped off the eye makeup that was smudged before redoing my eyeliner and eye shadow.

"So can I ask what made you want to do this?" Emily asked.

I paused for a moment before responding. "I honestly don't know."

"Well, when did it start?"

"Like the first time? It was probably when I was about eleven or twelve?" I responded.

"That long ago? And you've been dressing up and doing this ever since then?"

"Not like every day or anything, although sometimes I wish I could. It's usually just when I know I'll be alone."

"That's so sad." Emily said while touching up my mascara.

"I just don't want anyone to judge me or look at me different…" My eyes began tearing up again as I continued. "My family would hate me if they knew."

"Stop, you're going to make me cry." Emily said before putting the mascara away. "I'll redo your makeup again, but I'd rather see you happy."

A smile flashed across my face as I appreciated Emily's support.

"How about you tell me what you like to do when you get dressed up?" Emily said with a smile.

I took a couple of deep breaths as I thought about her question. "Honestly, by the time I do my hair and makeup, shave, and get dressed, there's not much time before someone will be coming home."

"But not tonight. What do you want to do?" Emily asked.

"I've always wanted to paint my nails." I said shyly.

Emily smiled, "Sit tight, I'll be right back."

Emily set out a few different colors of nail polish on my bed that she found in Gloria's room. I recognized the hot pink color as my sister's favorite and became uncomfortable.

"My sister is going to flip if she finds out I used her stuff…" I said.

"We borrow each other's stuff all the time. Trust me, it'll be ok." Emily responded.

"Well, the red one is cute, but I think I just want to start with the white color."

"Good choice. That'll look really good with your outfit."

Emily took my hand and led me downstairs to the kitchen. We sat at the table where she set out clear nail polish, nail polish remover, cotton balls, and the white-colored nail polish that I chose. I watched intently as Emily began with the base coat of clear nail polish on my left index finger.

"I thought you were painting them white?" I asked.

"I am, but you need to start with a base layer. I'll do another coat of this after we paint the color on." Emily responded.

"Oh, ok…" I said, feeling jittery.

"It's ok, I can remove it all later if you want. It's not permanent or anything."

"Ok good. I'm sorry, this all just makes me so nervous. I still can't believe I'm sitting here with you while I'm dressed like this."

"Just relax, I have a couple of gay friends at school." Emily responded.

"I'm not gay…" I snapped back.

"I'm sorry, I just meant…"

"It's ok, it's kind of confusing to me too. I mean, I still like girls, I just feel a need…or like I want to dress up like a girl sometimes."

"Yeah, I remember you dated that one girl for a while. What was her name?"

"Ashley…" I responded.

"Did she know you did this?" Emily asked as she finished up the base coat. I was shocked at how quickly she painted.

"Well, there was this one time. We were playing a board game, and I was teasing her because she like never wears dresses. So we made a bet that if I won, she would wear a dress to school every day for a month. And if I lost, I would put on a dress and high heels and dance like a girl. I kind of threw the game and made sure I lost, so we went to her room and she found a dress that kind of fit me. After I put on the sparkly pink dress and fit halfway into her shoes, she laughed at me while I danced to the radio station she picked. I guess I can't blame her for laughing at me, cause I kind of treated it like a joke too. But I just felt like she would never really take me seriously if I was honest with her."

Emily continued painting my nails with the white color as she listened and nodded along.

"We broke up a couple of weeks later over something stupid. I don't even remember what it was about now."

"Did she tell anyone else about what you guys did?" Emily asked.

"I don't know. I was always nervous she would tell my friends at school, but no one ever said anything to me. I just tried to bury it and pretend it didn't happen."

Emily put the white nail polish away after finishing the last nail. She waited for the nails to dry before continuing with the final top coat.

"Is she the only one you've ever dressed up with?" Emily asked.

"Until today, yeah…" I answered.

Emily looked me in the eye. "Your secret is safe with me."

"Thank you. This looks really good by the way." I said, while looking at my right hand.

"When you can't afford to get your nails done every month, you get a lot of practice."

I watched as Emily finished up the left hand and began cleaning up.

"You're going to need to let it dry for a few minutes. This is the quick dry stuff, so it shouldn't be too long."

I nodded my head as I stared down.

CHAPTER 5

I couldn't believe that I was looking at my own hands in front of me. Having my nails done made me feel put together in a way I hadn't experienced before. Shaving my legs, doing my makeup, and getting dressed all made me feel feminine, but my manicured nails made me feel like a real woman. I began tearing up again as I looked down.

"What's wrong? You don't like it?" Emily asked.

"No…They're perfect." I responded.

"Come here."

Emily pulled me in for another hug and held me tight. I embraced her and closed my eyes. After a few moments, I let go and stepped back.

"Do you wanna dance?" Emily asked.

A smile illuminated my face as I nodded yes in agreement.

I followed Emily to the living room, where we turned on the TV and found the pop station. Hearing a song that she loved, Emily turned the volume up high and began shaking her hips while throwing her arms up in the air.

Feeling nervous to shake my body in front of someone else, I watched for a few moments with my hands together in front of me. Emily turned toward me and dropped her hands to her side. After giving me a disappointed look, she stepped over and took my hands.

Emily began swaying back and forth in front of me while trying to get me to mimic her movements. As I began loosening up, I rocked my hips back and forth with the music. Bringing my hands up, Emily guided me as I twirled in front of her. The bottom half of my dress flared out all around me as I spun in the living room.

Time ceased to exist as we laughed and danced to several songs that played on the pop station. I finally felt free. Free of judgement, free of worrying what other people thought, free to just be myself and not have any worry in the world. Emily tried showing me some new moves as I laughed and did my best to follow along.

As I started to feel out of breath, I paused and sat on the couch while the music continued. Emily walked over to the TV and turned the volume down before sitting on the couch opposite of me.

"That was so much fun." I said while still catching my breath.

"You've got some moves." Emily complimented.

"Nothing like you…"

"Oh come on, I look like a giraffe that just learned how to walk." Emily laughed.

"Well I probably looked like a drunk flamingo." I responded.

We both laughed with each other as we slinked back on the couches.

"I'm so happy I came over here today." Emily said.

"Yeah, same here. I didn't know you were so cool." I responded.

"Thanks…" Emily said while rolling her eyes.

"No, I just meant…"

"I know what you meant. I'm just giving you a hard time." Emily said with a smile. "And seriously, if you ever need someone to talk to, you won't scare me away."

"I bet I could…" I answered.

"Try me…"

I paused for a moment before speaking. "So you know how I like to dress up like a girl…"

"Obviously."

"Well, there's one fantasy that I've always wanted to try…" I said.

"Yeah, what is it?"

I swallowed the saliva in my mouth as I started to get nervous. "I… uh…Never mind."

"What, you can't do that."

"Do what."

"Start to tell me something, then stop like that…We're way past you being shy. Spill it."

"It's just…it's kind of embarrassing."

Emily rolled her eyes again before staring at me intently.

"Ok fine. So you know how in movies and stories and stuff, there is like a girl that gets kidnapped and then someone has to come rescue her."

"Like a damsel in distress?" Emily chimed in.

"Yeah…I kind of like to imagine myself as the girl in that situation. Like I'm all dressed up as a princess, then I get tied up and I have to wait for someone to come rescue me."

"That is amazing! I love it!" Emily said while smiling.

"You don't think it's stupid?" I asked.

"Tons of girls have a fantasy where their prince charming comes and sweeps them off their feet."

"I'm not really a girl, though."

"But still, it's not that weird. I mean, if you want to hear something really strange, I have a fantasy where I'm like a doctor and someone comes in really messed up and I have to nurse them back to normal. We fall in love, have babies, and grow old together."

"That's not that weird. You're studying to be a nurse."

"I know, but how messed up is it that I want someone to be nearly dead so that I can save them and fall in love with them?"

"Ok, that is a little weird…" I chuckled.

"Yeah, what is normal." Emily said.

"Boring." I responded.

"Exactly. You know, I have some more time if you want to be the…" Emily used a dramatic voice to finish her sentence, *"damsel in distress."*

"What, are you serious?"

"Why wouldn't I be? Go to your room. I'll grab a couple things."

CHAPTER 6

I sat nervously on my bed as I waited for Emily to come upstairs. She appeared in my doorway a few minutes later with ropes and duct tape that she found in the garage.

"Are you ready?" Emily said with an evil grin.

I sat nervously and shook my head yes.

"This might be easier if you sat in a chair." Emily said.

Sitting up from the foot of my bed, I walked over to my desk in the corner of the room. I pulled out the wooden chair sitting partially under the desk and turned it around. As I sat down, Emily walked in front of me and set down the rope and tape.

"So what's the backstory?" Emily said as she began running rope around my legs.

"What do you mean?" I asked.

"Like what's your character? Were you a princess that was kidnapped by the king's enemies? Are you a movie star that is being held for ransom?"

"Oh…I liked the first one you said." I answered.

"Ok, so what's your princess name?"

"My princess name?"

"Yeah, I assume it isn't David." Emily said while laughing.

I chuckled with her while thinking. "I always liked the name Amber."

"Princess Amber. I like it." Emily said while tying off the knot around my legs. She grabbed my wrists and began tying the rope tightly around them in front of me.

"So princess Amber, you thought you could escape me." Emily said with an evil look on her face.

I tried to play along but couldn't act nearly as well as she did.

"Please, just let me go." I pleaded.

"Not until your father comes to his senses. Until he opens up trade for the north, you will be here a long, long time." Emily said as she tied off the knot holding my wrists together. She picked up the last rope and began running it around my torso, just below my chest. I sat up straight as she used the entire length of rope to coil it around me like a snake. After she finished wrapping it around my torso and arms, she tied it off in a knot behind my back.

I struggled against the rope for a few seconds before realizing I was actually stuck. With my wrists tied together and the rope around my body, there was no way to untie myself. With my legs tied together, the only thing I could possibly do was hop around my room.

Emily pulled off some tape and carefully placed it over my mouth. I closed my eyes and scrunched my face as she smoothed it out over my lips.

"There, you're all mine, princess."

I opened my eyes and stared at Emily. Feelings of nervousness and excitement came over me. I could feel the fluttering of butterflies in my stomach as I sat still on the chair.

"Now, it's time to..." Emily was cut off with her phone ringing. She put her finger up before looking down and seeing who it was. Emily gave a sigh before answering the phone.

"Hi mom." Emily answered.

"Right now? I thought dad was going to?"

"Are you sure?"

"Fine, I guess I'll be right there."

Emily hung up the phone and turned her attention back to me.

"I'm sorry, that was my mom. I have to go pick up my sister from dance." Emily said as she leaned down in front of me and reached for the rope.

I hung my head as she began loosening the knot. Emily paused as she looked up at me. Seeing the disappointment on my face, she let go of the rope.

"It'll only be fifteen minutes, tops. Do you want me to leave you until I come back?" Emily asked.

I looked into Emily's eyes and thought for a moment. Unable to think of another time that I might be able to do this, I shook my head yes.

"Are you sure?"

I shook my head yes again in response. Emily tightened the rope around my legs and stood up.

"The queen beckons my attention. You just sit tight, princess, while I'm away."

Emily smiled as she walked out of my room.

I looked out of my window and watched as Emily exited the house from the garage and closed it behind her. After getting in her car, she sat for a minute before backing out of the long driveway and pulling away down the street. As she disappeared from my sight, I turned my attention back to the rope tied around me.

CHAPTER 7

Sitting alone in my room, I squirmed and struggled against the rope. To my surprise, it wouldn't budge in the slightest. Although my arms were tied in front of me, I couldn't possibly reach the rope tied tightly around my body. I was able to reach down to my legs where I could've untied the rope around my ankles, but I decided to leave it.

As I struggled against the tape over my mouth, I quickly realized that with some movement of my jaw, I could open my mouth if I chose. Not wanting to ruin the experience, I moved my head down and smoothed the tape back over my lips with my hands. I was shocked that it was so easy to break the seal of the tape over my mouth. After years of seeing people in movies tied up and unable to speak from a single piece of tape over their mouth, I was disappointed to find out that it was just movie magic.

Sitting back in my chair, I closed my eyes and tried to take in the moment. I pulled against the rope around my wrists while kicking against the rope around my ankles. In my dress, high heels, and makeup, the feeling of struggling against my restraints was exhilarating. I wiggled my butt back and forth in my seat as I felt myself swelling up in my panties. After years of dreaming, I was finally living out one of my deepest fantasies. I was the damsel in distress, waiting to be rescued.

Bringing my hands to my middle, I found myself unable to reach my growing member. The most I could manage was to rub the rope around my wrists against the fabric of the dress. Fortunately, I didn't need much stimulation to continue feeling blood rush to my middle.

I kept my eyes closed tightly as I pulled against my

restraints and continued rubbing myself with the rope. My butt and crotch began tensing from the imminent release that was approaching. The only thing I could focus on was reaching this climax that I had been waiting for since morning. I could feel my abdomen tensing as the first drops leaked into my panties.

Small squeals escaped me as I began moving my hands up and down faster. The soft, soothing feeling of my dress and panties was becoming too much while I sat bound in my room. My breaths became shallow, as an explosion was so close that I could almost taste it. I leaned forward and pulled against all my restraints as liquid began rushing into my panties.

A wave of relief swept over me as one squirt after another filled my panties and dripped between my legs. I began breathing heavier as I rubbed every last drop of liquid out while keeping my eyes closed tightly. After a few minutes of intense pleasure, I regained my composure and fluttered my eyes open again.

As I looked around my room, I could feel myself slipping back into my male persona. My thoughts began focusing on what I had just done and not wanting Emily to find me sitting in my own mess. Typically, once I experienced a release, my attention would turn back to hiding this part of myself. I would undress and put away my female clothes until it was safe to bring it out again.

Bringing my focus back to the ropes tied around me, I started wiggling my body back and forth while hoping to find a weak point. Unfortunately, the ropes around my torso held tight with the knot behind my back. After a few minutes of struggling, I paused to regain my breath.

'How the hell am I going to get out of this?' I thought to myself.

I looked around my room, hoping to see something I could use to untie myself. To my dismay, nothing jumped out at me. As I glanced out the window to the front, something strange grabbed my attention.

"Where did that van come from?" I thought to myself.

At some point while I was struggling against the ropes and pleasuring myself, a white work van with no windows or markings had pulled into the driveway and parked in front of the garage.

"Is that Emily?" I thought to myself, "her dad does have a plumbing company...but why would she be driving one of the vans?"

While trying to figure out who the mysterious van belonged to, I heard voices echoing from downstairs.

My heart began racing and my eyes went wide as I heard footsteps making their way up the stairs. I twisted my body back and forth, trying my best to wiggle out of the ropes. Straining with everything I had, I flexed my arms and tensed my shoulders.

Hearing a noise at my door, I looked up to see a man wearing jeans, a black face mask, and a dark hoodie with the hood up. Only his eyes, forehead, and hands were exposed as he froze and peered at me. Locking eyes with his, he looked equally surprised to see someone in the house. I remained frozen as another man wearing similar attire walked up next to him and whispered. "What are you doing?"

The man who had been standing in the doorway pointed in my direction in response.

As both men stared at me unblinking, I quickly brought my legs up and began untying the knot around my ankles. The men saw what I was doing and lunged toward me. One grabbed my arms while the other grabbed my legs and held me down. I opened my mouth and broke the seal of the tape over my lips.

"Help! Someone help!" I yelled.

One of the men grabbed the tape sitting next to me and began running it around my head. After wrapping it around at least three times, I found myself unable to open my mouth or get another word out.

Using the duct tape, the two men began wrapping it around the rope that was tied around my ankles and wrists. Once they had reinforced the rope, they used the rest of the roll to tape me to the chair that I was sitting on. I squirmed back and forth as one of the men held me down and the other continued running the tape around my torso and the backrest of the chair.

Seeing that I was unable to escape, the two men stepped

back and began catching their breath. They made eye contact with each other before stepping out of the room and whispering in the hall. With how low they kept their voices, I couldn't decipher what they were discussing with each other. I continued wiggling in my restraints and trying to break free while they peeked in on me every couple of minutes.

After several minutes of what sounded like intense deliberation, one of the men stepped into my room and watched me while the other ran downstairs. I looked down at the floor while the man sat on my bed and stared at the wall in front of him. We sat in silence as I waited for what was next.

CHAPTER 8

I could hear one of the burglars moving things around and unplugging cords on the TV in the living room while his accomplice sat with me. Although they had broken into my house, I could sense that I wasn't in any real danger. In fact, there was something very familiar about both of them.

Neither would look into my eyes for very long, and the one guarding me made sure to keep his head turned away as much as possible. He would glance at me to make sure I was still secure in my bondage, but quickly look away. I turned my attention out the window as I sat and waited for them to rob my family and leave.

Looking out the window next to me, I stared blankly while thoughts raced through my head. As I watched the trees sway in the wind, I did my best to relax and try to collect my thoughts.
'How the hell did this happen?' I thought to myself. 'First Emily shows up, then two burglars. And why do I feel like I've seen them before? I could've sworn I've seen them somewhere. Those eyes…' My thoughts were interrupted by the sight of a car pulling back into the driveway. Emily had returned.

The small red car pulled into the driveway, but stopped while still halfway in the street. Looking over to the man guarding me, I could see that he was oblivious to the vehicle that had just showed up. He continued staring straight ahead at the wall while actively avoiding any eye contact.

I looked back out the window and strained to try to see what Emily was doing. Nearly seventy meters away, I could just barely make out her talking with someone on the phone. She remained in her car as she brought the phone down and made another call.

After a few minutes, she slowly pulled out of the driveway and drove down the street. I looked back at the man sitting in my room to find him completely unaware of the fact that someone had pulled into the driveway and left. As I looked back out of the window, I watched as Emily parked on the street across from my neighbor's house and turned off her vehicle.

Turning my attention back to what was happening inside of my house, I listened for the intruder, who was downstairs. It sounded like he had disconnected the TV and stereo system and was now making his way through the various rooms of my family's house. The man in my room walked over to the hallway and stood just outside of my doorway. He peeked in and checked on me every couple of minutes while watching downstairs for his partner.

As I glanced outside my window again, I noticed flashing lights making their way down the street. I watched intently as they came to my driveway and three police cars pulled in. I could hear the garage door close as five police officers stepped out of their vehicles and drew their weapons. Shouting echoed through the house as the man downstairs ran up to my room and yelled at his partner.

"What the hell are you doing?" One yelled to the other.

"What?" He responded.

"The fucking police just showed up!" He screamed.

The other man stepped into my room and looked out the window to see what was happening.

"Oh shit, the police are here."

"No shit. Why weren't you keeping watch?"

"I was!"

"The hell you were! What are we going to do now?"

"I don't know. We could run out the back."

"My van's out front. I can't just leave it. They'll know I was here."

"Look, I don't know, I just…I don't wanna go to jail."

"Yeah, well then, think of something."

"It was your idea to come here. You think of something."

I could see one of the men rub their face as they were trying to control their aggravation.

"What if we send David out and sneak out the back while they're distracted?"

"My van is still out front."

"We'll figure it out later. Let's just get out of here."

'Send David out?' I thought to myself. 'How do they know my name?'

"That's a terrible idea."

"I'm all ears if you've got anything better…"

One of the men took a deep breath before stepping in front of me and crouching down to my level. As he pulled the face mask down, I finally figured out why he was so familiar.

CHAPTER 9

'Michael?' I thought to myself.

"Look David, I'm going to be honest with you here. I don't know what the fuck you're doing here dressed up in your sister's clothes. I thought your whole family was going to grandpa's this weekend. You know Bobby and I have been having a tough time the last few months..."

"Why the fuck did you say my name?!" Bobby yelled from the other side of the room.

"Just shut up." Michael yelled before continuing. "I won't tell anyone about this if you just help us out. We can untie you and let you go, just please..." Michael put his head down and brought his hand over his face.

"If another grandkid ends up in jail, it's going to kill grandpa. I'm begging you. Please help us."

Michael pulled out a knife and began cutting the tape around my legs and wrists. Once the tape was free, he untied the ropes and helped release the tape around my mouth.

I remained speechless as I stood up and turned toward the window.

I could feel my cousins becoming very uncomfortable as I contemplated what to do next.

Bobby nudged his brother as he whispered, "We have to go".

Micheal grunted before turning back to me. "David, what are you going to do?"

I took a deep breath and paused for a few more moments. The suspense must have been eating at my cousins, but I still hadn't decided what I was going to do.

"David..." Michael said again.

"Michael, we have to go." Bobby pressed again.

"Shut up!" He snapped back. "David, what are you going to do?"

I took another deep breath and responded calmly. "I'm going to walk outside and tell the police exactly what happened."

I began moving toward the door before Michael stepped in front of me.

"Don't you want to change? I can help keep this a secret if you cover for us…"

"No, I'm done. Now move." I said plainly.

"David, what are saying?"

"Step aside." I said firmly.

Michael sighed before stepping away. I walked out of my room and slowly made my way down the stairs. My heart beat out of my chest as I approached the front door and stopped in front of it. I put my hand on the doorknob and looked behind me.

My cousins ran down the stairs behind me and headed for the back door to the patio. I shook my head before opening the door and stepping outside. The police shouted at me as I walked down the sidewalk and made my way toward them with my hands up. I could hear Emily yelling behind them as I took one step after another.

Feeling the cool air against my bare legs and hearing the sound of my heels against the concrete, I felt outside of myself. For the first time in my life, I stepped outside while crossdressed. I stopped just a few feet away from the police and closed my eyes while anxiety filled my stomach. I could feel my breath speeding up as my head became dizzy. It felt like I could faint at any moment as I crouched down to the ground and put my hands over my head.

Emily ran over and put her arms around me as a panic attack set in. I fell onto my hands and knees and kept my eyes closed tightly while a few police ran by me into the house. Two police officers walked up and stood beside me as I tried my best to compose myself.

"David, hey. It's ok!" Emily said while trying to comfort me. "You're safe now, it's ok!"

Hearing her voice and feeling her embrace had a way of bringing me back to reality. I fluttered my eyes open and turned my attention to her.

"Are there still people in the house?" One of the police asked.

"I think they ran out the back." I responded in a breathy voice.

"Don't worry, we'll find them." He responded.

"It's ok, I know who they are…they're not dangerous, they're just stupid."

"What are their names?" The police officer asked.

"They're my cousins, Michael and Bobby Valero. They were going to rob the house while my parents were away."

"Why don't you come with me and sit down?" The police officer said.

Emily and I followed him to his car, where he let us sit in the back with the door open. Emily kept her arm around my shoulder as I twiddled my thumbs and stared at my feet. After a half an hour of waiting, I could hear one of the police announce on the radio that they caught the intruders. I sighed in relief when I heard that no one was injured.

CHAPTER 10

Once the police had taken Michael and Bobby into custody, they took them to the police station while Emily and I went back into the house. Emily sat with me while I gave a statement to the police as to what had happened. I told them that they did not harm me and that I was free to leave when I asked. When the police had everything they needed, they offered to leave a police officer stationed out front until my parents returned. With Emily by my side, I told them that they could leave.

Emily sat in the living room as I walked upstairs to my room and removed my panties that had been soiled. As I threw my panties on the floor and began pulling up my dress, I froze in place. Thinking about how many people saw me dressed up today, I started contemplating how I could possibly keep this a secret from my family. They had called several times, but I had not answered them yet. Emily had let my family know everything that had happened and they informed me that they were on their way home.

I let the dress fall back to my knees before putting on a fresh pair of panties and sitting on the bed.

'What am I going to tell them?' I thought to myself. 'I know Emily would keep it a secret, but I couldn't trust Michael or Bobby as far as I could throw them. And all the police saw me dressed like this. There is no way my family won't find out'

I started having trouble swallowing my saliva as my breathing became heavier. My head became light, and I fell to the floor on my hands and knees. I could feel tears welling up as I closed my eyes tightly.

I jumped as I felt a hand touch my back and start rubbing.

"It's ok, I'm here." Emily said, trying to comfort me. "What's wrong?"

I swallowed the saliva building in my mouth and tried to get the words out.

"Everyone is going to find out." I said with tears in my eyes.

"I won't tell anyone." She responded.

"I'm not worried about you. My cousins are assholes. There's no way they're going to keep their mouths shut after I turned them in."

"You never know, they might surprise you. But if you are really worried, maybe it's time to finally be honest."

"They're going to hate me. And judge me. I can't do this…"

"Who? Your family? They'll love you no matter what. You should know that."

"I don't know, they…they won't understand."

"Look, I'm not going anywhere. If you need help telling them, I'm here for you."

The sound of the garage door opening pierced through me as I sat on the floor.

"Oh my god they're here." I said with panic in my voice. "Oh my god, oh my god. What am I gonna do…"

"Just, sit right here. I'll go downstairs and talk to them. You can just come downstairs whenever you're ready, ok?"

I swallowed the saliva building up again and shook my head in agreement.

I listened as Emily walked downstairs and greeted my sister in the kitchen.

"Oh my god, are you ok? What happened?" My sister asked while my parents walked in behind her.

"Yeah, I'm fine." Emily responded. "I saw there was a van in the driveway when I came over to check on David. When I saw someone with a mask loading a TV into the back, I called the cops and waited on the other side of the street."

"Where's David? Is he ok?" My mom asked.

"Yeah, he's ok, he's just upstairs resting still." Emily answered.

"He must have been scared to death!" My mom asserted.

"I think he was, but he's ok now." Emily said.

"I'm going to go check on him…" My mom said before getting cut off by Emily.

"Actually, he's going to come downstairs in a few minutes…he has something to tell you all."

"What?" My dad asked.

"Yeah what?" Gloria asked as well.

"He uh…well he…I uh…He should probably just tell you himself…"

"What are talking about? I'm going to go check on my son…" My mom said while taking a few steps toward the stairs.

"No, just wait…" Emily said while stepping in front of her

"Emily…" My sister snapped.

"Gloria…"

"What is going on, Emily?" My dad said, sounding aggravated.

"Don't get upset at Emily." I said while taking a step into the kitchen while wearing my dress and high heels.

CHAPTER 11

The room fell completely silent as my family stared at me with eyes wide open. I took a few deep breaths as I tried to control my anxiety that was creeping up yet again. As I swallowed the saliva in my mouth, I could feel my breathing speeding up uncontrollably and another panic attack about to set in. My knees began to wobble before Emily slid next to me and put her arm around my shoulder.

"David…" My dad said slowly, "Why are you wearing your sister's clothes?"

"Did you dress him up like this?" My mom asked Emily aggressively. "What did you do to my little boy?"

"She didn't do this…" I said with a crack in my voice.

"Then what's going on?" My dad asked with his arms crossed.

I looked over at Emily, then hung my head. "I wasn't sick this morning…"

"David, go get changed and we'll…" I cut my mom off and continued.

"I don't want to go change my clothes. I pretended to be sick so I could stay home and wear this. I've been doing this for a while and I'm just starting to get so tired of pretending to be something I'm not."

"What are saying? Are you like gay or something?" My sister asked.

"It's not about that." I answered.

"Do you want to be a girl?" My mom asked.

"No…I mean, I don't think so. I just like girly clothes and feel like I need to wear them sometimes. It probably doesn't make any sense to you guys…"

"No...it doesn't." My dad blurted.

I took a deep breath before continuing. "You guys were going to find out sooner or later. I just wanted to be the one to tell you. I'm sorry for lying to you guys."

A tear formed in my eye and ran down my cheek as I hung my head and waited in silence for another round of questions. After some of the longest seconds of my life, I looked up to see my mom and sister approaching me. Emily joined my mother and sister as they gave a group hug and held me tight. I closed my eyes and took in the warmth and comfort that I was receiving. My eyes began tearing uncontrollably as I wept in their arms.

We stood in the kitchen with each other for a few minutes before Emily let go first, followed by my mother, then my sister. As I looked over at my dad, I could see that his arms were still crossed with an aggravated look on his face. I stood frozen in place as I waited for his reaction.

As we stood in silence, my mother looked over at my dad and nodded in my direction. He stood still for a few more seconds before he shook his head and walked out of the room. Everyone jumped as we heard his bedroom door slam behind him. I could feel myself shaking as I stood next to Emily and my sister.

"I'm sorry. I'm sure he'll come to his senses sooner or later." My mom said before giving me a kiss and following my dad to their room.

I wiped the tears from my eyes as I tried to preserve the makeup that was running down my cheeks.

"Do you need another touch up?" Emily asked.

I nodded my head yes as I held back more tears.

"Can I help?" My sister asked.

I looked over at her with a smile and nodded yes.

Emily, Gloria, and I walked upstairs to my sister's room and closed the door behind us. As I sat on the floor, Gloria pulled out her makeup bag and set it in front of me. Emily began cleaning off my eyes as Gloria prepared the eye shadow, eyeliner, and mascara. "I had no idea you were into this kind of stuff." Gloria said, while sitting directly in front of me.

"I didn't feel like I could tell anyone." I responded.

"You know you can trust me, right?"

"Yeah, I know, it just felt so embarrassing."

"How long have you known?" Gloria asked Emily.

"I literally just found out today." She answered with her hands up as if at gunpoint.

Gloria gave Emily a look as she held an eyeliner pen in Emily's direction.

"She's telling the truth. She walked in on me today when she came to check on me." I informed Emily.

"I bet you're really upset I had her come over here." Gloria said.

"You know, I'm actually happy she stopped by." I said while smiling at Emily.

"So are you going to be dressing like this everyday now? Is that what this is all about?" Gloria asked.

"I don't know about that." I answered. "I still like being a guy. I just feel like dressing like a girl sometimes. It's like, sometimes I'm David, and sometimes I'm Amber."

"Amber?" My sister asked.

"I don't know. It's just a name we came up with today. It's probably stupid."

"No...It's cute." My sister said.

I looked down as I felt embarrassed.

"I have to ask you something and please be honest, ok? Has 'Amber' ever come in here and worn my clothes?" Gloria asked.

I swallowed the saliva in my mouth and paused for a moment.

"Well that's a yes." Gloria said.

"What! I didn't say that."

"You didn't have to."

I kept my eyes on the floor as I sat still.

"Don't worry, I'm not upset. It's just, if you need to go shopping or something, you can ask me to come with. I can help you if you need something."

"That goes for me too." Emily chimed in.

"Really?" I said, surprised.

"Yeah, just don't hide anything like this from me. I want to be there for you."

"Thank you."

Emily and Gloria cleaned up my makeup and touched up my eyes as we sat and chatted in my sister's room. I finally felt at home as we had a deep conversation with each other. Despite how amazing my sister was being, I still felt a pit in my stomach from the way my dad reacted. I couldn't help feeling my anxiety creep back up when footsteps made their way upstairs to Gloria's room.

After a knock on the door, Gloria popped up and answered it.

"Your father wants you guys to come downstairs." My mother informed.

"We're not going to come down there so he can yell at Amber." My sister said.

"Amber?" My mom asked.

"Yeah, that's what he wants to be called when he's dressed like... this..." my sister informed.

"Ok..." my mom sighed, "Amber, please come downstairs."

Gloria turned to me and waited to see what I would do. After taking a deep breath, I stood to my heels and followed my mom downstairs to the living room with Emily and Gloria one step behind.

CHAPTER 12

My father sat on the couch with his arms crossed as we walked into the living room. I stepped through the doorway and stood against the wall on the opposite side of the room while my mom sat next to my father on the couch. Gloria and Emily stood next to me in the doorway as we waited for the screaming to begin.

"David…" My father said while keeping his gaze on the floor in front of him. "Your mother and I had a long talk and…well I'm not sure where to start."

I clenched my stomach as I looked down at the floor. My mother put her arm around my father as she continued for him. "Look David…Or should I say, Amber?" My father's head turned toward my mom with a confused look on his face. "We just want to understand what this is all about?"

"What do you mean?" I asked.

"Well, do you want to be a man or a woman?" My mom asked.

I left my eyes on the floor as I thought about the question for a few moments. "Why do I have to choose? Why can't I just dress how I feel?" I asked.

"We can't stop you from dressing however you want. We just want to protect you from what people might say." My mom responded.

"I don't really care what people say anymore. If people find out that I wear dresses and makeup sometimes, I don't really care. I'm still going to be me and do the things I like to do."

"And you really like wearing girly dresses and…makeup?" My dad asked.

My breath felt shallow as I answered, "Yeah, sometimes."

My father's face went solemn as tears formed in his eyes. "Why?

What did I do wrong?"

Feeling extremely uncomfortable, I was unable to look at my parents for more than a second at a time. I glanced over periodically and kept my eyes to the right of where they were sitting.

"If I could tell you why I like the things I do, I would. It's not like there is some switch that I can turn off. It's just who I am. And if you can't accept that…" my eyes began tearing as I continued, "I just don't have anything else to talk about right now."

"Honey, we care about you." My mom asserted.

I kept my eyes on the wall to my right as a tear began crawling down my cheek.

"We both care about you…" my mom said while nudging my dad.

He remained quiet as tears made their way down his cheek.

"Can you at least just tell us if we'll ever see our David again?" My mom asked calmly.

"Of course, I'm not going anywhere. I just feel like I need to do some self reflecting and find out who I really am." I responded.

"Look, I'm not going to pretend to understand, but I do want you to know that we are here for you. It just might take some time for everyone to get used to it." My mom said sincerely.

My father sat next to her looking like he could break down sobbing at any moment.

I tried to accept my mother's support, but felt distracted by my dad's disapproval. "Thank you mom. I really…really appreciate it." My mother looked over at my father and put her arm around him. As she held him tight, she nodded for Gloria, Emily, and me to leave the room. I nodded to my mom before walking out behind the girls.

As we walked back up to Gloria's room, I felt a pit in my stomach. It was clear that my father didn't accept what I was wearing. After seeing the look on his face of betrayal and regret, I couldn't help but feel a massive weight pulling me down.

I stopped on the steps and took a deep breath. Gloria and Emily turned around from the top of the stairs and called back to me.

"Aren't you coming?" Emily asked.

I breathed heavily as I thought about what I should do. 'Just because he wants to ignore what's happening and try to hide from it, that doesn't mean I have to.'

I spun around and marched back down the stairs. As I turned the corner to the living room, I could see that my mom and dad had stood up and started walking to the doorway that I stepped inside of. My father's face was of complete shock as he saw me return.

We stared at each other for a moment before I ran forward and embraced him. His body felt stiff as he stood uncomfortably with my arms around him. With my eyes closed and head against his shoulder, I whispered to him, "I still love you."

I held on for a few seconds before releasing my grip. The tenseness that I initially felt had subsided, and he took his turn to hug me. I accepted his warm embrace as we stood in the living room, sharing one of the most significant moments of my life. "I still love you, too." He said softly.

After letting go of each other, I stepped away and ran upstairs to Gloria and Emily. They almost didn't believe me when I told them what had just happened. But, as the days and weeks passed, everyone could see that my dad was finally on my side.

Thank you for reading!

If you enjoyed this book or any of the other books in this series, please consider leaving a review. Five star reviews are extremely helpful and let me know to continue writing stories like these. To stay up to date with new releases, please follow me on amazon and instagram at jane_doe_feminization_author.

Thank you so much for the support and for taking time out of your day to read one of my many stories.

-Jane Doe

BOOKS BY THIS AUTHOR

Black(E)Mail

Have you been keeping your sissy life a secret? How far would you go to keep your friends and family from knowing you're a closeted crossdresser?

In 'Black(E)Mail', we meet a young man who still lives with his very conservative parents. Forced to keep the sissy side of himself a secret, he spends many late nights browsing videos and stories involving forced feminization. When a mysterious email pops up in his mailbox stating that they know his secret, he deletes it and brushes it off. When another identical email pops up again, he becomes agitated and deletes it a second time. Within a few moments, his computer is spammed with thousands of emails from the same address. He restarts his computer and powers it back up to find emails popping up by the thousands. After accidentally clicking on one of the messages pouring in, he finds a video from his webcam showing him pleasuring himself to a forced feminization video. The message informs him that if he doesn't follow their orders, the video will be messaged to everyone on his contact list. Not wanting his secret exposed, he follows their first order to remove all of his underwear from his drawer and throw it out the window to the front yard. Once he completes the task, they inform him that his next task will be given in the morning. When he wakes up to discover that all of his belongings disappeared from the front yard, he begins to get anxious and believes that he is being watched. As tasks continue being given to the young man, he is ordered to gather the supplies that he will need to crossdress as a woman. After collecting his own pair of panties and bra, he must purchase a red dress and matching high heels. With each task he is given, it becomes increasingly difficult to turn back or quit. Along the way, the young sissy is made to have his nails, hair, and makeup done professionally at a studio. Enjoy this fast-paced story that takes a secretive young man and turns him into a reluctant feminized sissy.

Maid To Be Mine

Have you ever dreamt of becoming a sissy maid for a dominating woman? Do you wish that your significant other would help you begin a new career as a full time sissy maid?

'Maid to be mine' explores the sissy maid lifestyle from the perspective of a woman who is learning about it for the first time. After the protagonist's boyfriend loses his job and goes on unemployment, she allows him to move into her apartment to save some money. When she comes home to dirty dishes, an unmade bed, and crumbs all over the carpet, she decides that something needs to change. While discussing the chores around the house, her boyfriend confides that he has a fantasy about becoming a sissy maid that cooks and cleans for his mistress. Being brand new to the subject of sissies and forced feminization, she begins doing some research and reading stories on the web. Intrigued by the idea, she gives the female led relationship a try. She quickly learns that her sissy needs a set of rules to follow so that he fulfills his duties properly. On her way home from work, she purchases new panties and bras to replace his dirty old male underwear. To test if he is serious about the new dynamic in their relationship, she orders the new sissy maid to shave all of his body hair. After throwing away all of his old male underwear and replacing it with panties and bras, she provides a maid's uniform that he must wear at all times around the house. While locked up in chastity and under the tight control of his new mistress, the sissy maid excels in his new role. When she tells her girlfriend about her new sissy maid, her girlfriend jokingly asks to have him clean her house to make some extra money. She happily agrees and begins sending her new sissy maid to cook and clean for her friends a few days a week. As you read along, it becomes clear how much attention a sissy requires and why they need an attentive and dominating mistress.

Becoming The Girl Of His Dreams

Have you ever had a sissy dream that felt so real that you couldn't distinguish it from reality? Have you ever wished that your dreams would become your new reality?
In 'Becoming the Girl of His Dreams', we meet a kind hearted closeted crossdresser who works at a diner. The protagonist has a strange encounter with a mysterious woman who informs him that all of his dreams will come true. After brushing off the comment as some sort of vague encouragement, he returns home and falls into a deep sleep. In his dream, his nails are painted bright pink and become much longer and more feminine. When he awakes the next morning, he is shocked to find his nails matching what he saw in his dream. Thinking that someone is pulling a prank on him, he tries to hide his nails while at work and figure it out later. With each passing night, he continues dreaming that he is being turned into a woman and finding those dreams manifesting in real life. From every bit of body hair magically vanishing from his body to a set of DD boobs appearing on his chest, he soon finds himself unrecognizable as the man he once was. His hair turns blonde and grows a foot over night and permeant makeup is painted on his face that will not come off. Unable to process the changes in his fragile male psyche, he denies what is happening and tries to fight against the female dominator that keeps appearing in his dreams. Will the sissy find a way to reverse the changes or have to learn how to live as the woman that he has always dreamt of becoming?

His New Toy

Have you ever wondered what it would be like to be the sissy lover to a rich, powerful, and sexy man? Have you ever fantasized about being a submissive sissy and crossdressing every day for the man of your dreams?

Let me introduce you to a young man that is about to explore every sissy's dream in 'His New Toy'. Having been out of luck in the dating scene with women, Ray decides to finally branch out and look for a man that will allow him to explore his innermost desires. After coming in contact with a man named Conner Wellington on the internet, Ray is invited to Conner's home to live as his sissy lover. Ray can't believe he isn't dreaming when he hears the three requirements in the proposition. He must submit to complete feminization of his body and appearance. Ray must act as femininely as possible at all times. And lastly, he must follow any and all of Conner's instructions. If he agrees to the proposal, everything he would ever need would be provided for him. After agreeing to move in with Conner, he is given a room with a closet full of dresses, skirts, high heels, bras, panties, and all the lingerie he could dream of. Ray is in sissy heaven as he transforms into the woman of his dreams through breast augmentation and facial reconstructive surgeries. The new sissy becomes fixated on Conner and finding ways to win his heart. As they explore their new relationship, the sissy is introduced to a part of the BDSM world that she didn't know existed. The sissy must learn to accept a chastity cage while remaining plugged at all times. While experiencing tie ups and gags, every button is pressed to make the sissy squeal. Enjoy the spicy romance as this sissy gets what she deserves.

His Favorite Toy

Have you ever fantasized about serving a rich and powerful man as his sissy lover? Do you wish you could wear a French maid's dress, stockings, high heels, and makeup everyday while serving the man of your dreams?

In 'His Favorite Toy', we meet a sissy named Bridget who lives on a private island with her master, Conner. While living on the island, Bridget performs the duties of a maid while servicing any and all of her master's needs. With a special room full of tie ups and gags, Bridget is always kept on her toes wondering when she might be ravaged next. When a new maid named Rachel arrives on the island, Bridget takes it upon herself to mentor the new sissy and show her the ropes. As they begin to bond and form a unique relationship of their own, they start to realize that something has changed on the island. Although they continue to fool around and explore BDSM in their love making sessions with Conner, it becomes clear that something is bothering the man of their dreams. Embark on a journey to the Caribbean where we experience a steamy love triangle between two sissies and their devoted master.

Their New Doll

Have you ever fantasied about being trained as a proper sissy? Do you wish that two beautiful and strong mistresses would force you into submission as they explore their BDSM fantasies with you?

In 'Their New Doll', we see the world through the eyes of Conner Wellington, a billionaire who owns homes in New York City and the Caribbean. Using his wealth and power, Conner has devoted his life to seeking out submissive sissies and helping them feminize themselves. Providing the best treatment that money can buy, Conner invites young men to come and live with him, while they transition into the person they always dreamed of becoming. When they complete their transition, he either finds them a new home, or provides them with enough money that they can begin their new life anywhere in the world.

After years of philanthropic work, Conner can't help but feel like there is something missing in his life. As he is discussing his mental health with his long-time friend, Jennifer, he realizes that it is time to finally care for himself. Instead of living as the dominant man over his two sissy companions, Rachel and Bridget, they decide to switch roles and give Conner the same treatment he gave to his sissies. With the high heel on the other foot, he quickly realizes that the sissy lifestyle isn't as easy as he expected. As his body transitions, Conner experiences the BDSM lifestyle as a submissive and must learn to accept that his mistresses are now in complete control of every aspect of his life. When Rachel and Bridget begin to disagree about how they should treat their submissive servant, Conner finds himself in a love triangle, where both are competing for his love and affection. This steamy romance will keep you on the edge as you explore tie-ups, gags, sex doll suits, plugs, strap-ons, submissive training and much, much more.

She's Such A Witch

Have you ever fantasized about waking up in the body of a real-life French maid? Do you wish you could shed your male identity and become a beautiful, delicate female that is the object of everyone's sexual desire?

'She's Such a Witch' follows a man in his late twenties who keeps his crossdressing a secret, except for one day a year on Halloween. When a mysterious witch moves in next door and discovers his crossdressing secret, she begins to toy with him and telepathically whisper thoughts in his ear. As he tries to convince himself that he doesn't believe in magic, he ignores the witch's commands and falls under her spell. After waking up and discovering that he is inhabiting the body of a French woman who can't speak a word of English, he realizes just how powerful the witch is. She informs him that his life as a male is finished and he will be starting a new job as a maid. Instead of attending his neighbor's annual Halloween party as one of the guests, he will now serve the guests and make sure that everyone is satisfied. Dressed in a provocative black-and-white uniform with stockings and high-heeled booties, the protagonist quickly becomes the center of attention at the party. Although he is hesitant to test out his new body parts, his new instincts take over as he begins to crave the touch of a strong, muscular companion. After experiencing feelings that he didn't know existed, the protagonist is torn between what they thought they wanted and what they now desire. Will the young man find a way to reverse the spell or remain under the clutches of an immortal witch forever?

Sissy In Training

Does the thought of wearing latex and being trained as a submissive sissy excite you? Do you wish you could find someone to tie you up and make you feel like a real submissive?

In 'Sissy in Training', we meet a young sissy crossdresser named Demi and her best friend who goes by the name Brandi. While they are out at their favorite bar one evening, they meet a devilishly handsome man and his partner. The couple self describes as a master and dominatrix who "like to show girls like them a good time." Although Brandi is turned off by their proposal, Demi finds herself curious and excited about spending the night with the alluring man. Upon arrival at the power couple's home, Demi experiences the BDSM world in a way that she never knew existed. Over the course of the evening, Demi finds herself being pushed to her limits as she is dominated, controlled, and trained by the master and dominatrix. As it becomes later in the evening, Demi starts to wonder when or if they ever plan on letting her go. With a gag in her mouth and her arms tied tightly behind her, she is at the complete mercy of these two aggressive and sensual people. Feeling a mixture of excitement, fear, arousal, and anxiety, Demi can't seem to figure out what will come next. Take a journey with Demi as she is dominated and becomes a 'Sissy in Training'.

It's Hard Being A Sissy Housewife

Do you wish that you were married to a loving, understanding, and open-minded woman who would allow you to become a sissy housewife while they support both of you?

In 'It's Hard Being a Sissy Housewife', we meet a young couple with an unconventional love life. The husband enjoys crossdressing and playing the role of a submissive sissy while his wife takes on a dominating and aggressive persona. During their role playing, his outfits include high heels, short skirts or dresses, and plenty of makeup while his wife dresses in alluring lingerie and high heel stilettos of her own. As she shouts orders to her "little sissy", she makes sure that he acts girly and provocatively throughout their roleplaying. Once they have their fun and have both fulfilled their urges, they return to their heteronormative roles until the next week, when they will role play again. Although the protagonist enjoys crossdressing on the weekends and feels fulfillment from their love life, there is always a desire for more. After an eventful week where he finds himself out of a job and in possession of a small fortune, he decides to take some time off and become a sissy housewife for an entire week. On the very first day, instead of his wife returning to a clean home, the sink is full of dirty dishes, the floors need vacuuming, and the bed is still unmade. Frustrated with her lazy sissy housewife, she begins using a mistress manual that gives explicit instructions on how to train an unruly sissy. Following the first rule of the book, she requires him to wear a chastity cage full time and forbids him from removing it. With his manhood locked away, a strong desire is planted in his consciousness to please his mistress at all costs. As the week progresses, he begins to slip deeper and deeper into the sissy housewife role and starts to question if he can ever turn back. Find out who enjoys the new power structure in their relationship more while experiencing how hard it is when you are a sissy housewife.

Life In Her Heels

Have you ever wondered what it would be like to experience life as women have experienced throughout human history? To be told what you can wear, where you can go, and what you are allowed to do with your body?

In 'Life in Her Heels', the patriarchy is turned upside down when a charismatic female leader is voted into the White House. Running a campaign based on putting men and women on equal footing, the new leader of the country is voted into office, with a large majority in both chambers of Congress. To right the wrongs of human history, the new leadership puts laws into place that force men to experience what women have endured throughout the history of the world. The protagonist of the story finds himself living through this historic moment and must adhere to the new rules as they are written. While living with his wife, the young man must follow the new federal dress codes by turning in his pants for skirts and shoes for high heels. He and his wife are assigned new jobs that greatly alter the power structure in their home and finances. When his new job requires him to alter his body, he struggles with the changes that are occurring and how to express what is happening to him. As he slowly changes from a man to a feminized sissy, it starts to become impossible to hide his growing "assets". After an incident where he is unfairly blamed for initiating an encounter with someone in his apartment building, he is put on house arrest and required to wear a chastity belt at all times. Eventually, the protagonist becomes unrecognizable to the man he once was and must come to terms with his new life as a submissive sissy to his wife who now owns him.

Past The Point Of No Return

Have you ever wondered what it would be like to be turned into a real life sissy whore? To be completely feminized, chastised, and made to serve a mistress and master?

In the story 'Past the Point of No Return', we meet a young man who is curious to explore his sissy tendencies. Although he enjoys dressing and acting feminine when given the opportunity, he has never stepped out while en fem until one fateful night.

After receiving a phishing email from a mysterious dominatrix, he is asked to meet up at a local motel. Thinking with his other head, he decides to drive to the location given while dressed and made up as he was requested. While wearing a little black dress, high-heeled pumps, fishnet stockings, and a matching set of bra and panties, he meets the gorgeous woman who invited him. The woman informs him that she would like to tie him up during their session and he agrees promptly. Once he is bound, gagged, and unable to escape, the woman milks the sissy until he is completely dry. After locking the sissy into a steel chastity cage, the woman calls for two burly men who come and kidnap the scared sissy. The young man is taken to a facility where he is given a breast enhancement and facial reconstructive surgery. When he is transported to his new home, he is trained and hypnotized to be a submissive sissy slut that is eager to serve. Throughout the story, elements of forced feminization, Feminization surgery, Bimbofication, sissy hypnotism, sissy prostitution, and bondage are all explored. If you are still reading this and haven't been scared off, this may be the book for you.

The Queen Of Sissy Hypnosis

Are you curious about how powerful sissy hypnosis can be? Do you wish that the Queen of Sissy Hypnosis would put you under her spell and turn you into a completely feminized sissy servant that obeys every command?

In 'The Queen of Sissy Hypnosis', we meet a young couple who hires a sissy hypnosis expert to come stay with them. With strict bondage and constant hypnosis, the reluctant sissy is transformed from the inside out as his self image begins to reflect what he has always desired to become. The Queen of Sissy Hypnosis teaches the inexperienced mistress how she should treat her submissive sissy in order to maintain her dominance over him. After giving him a feminine name that reinforces his new identity as a submissive sissy, he is put on a strict routine that involves maintaining a hairless body, wearing a full face of makeup, styling his hair femininely, cleaning the house, and most importantly, 16 hours of daily hypnosis. The young sissy is broken by his new mistress as she teaches him how to orgasm while locked in a chastity cage. To cement his role as a submissive sissy for life, the young man is paraded down his street while fully made up and dressed as a slutty maid while collared and leashed. Enjoy this hot and steamy romance as we discover how powerful sissy hypnosis can be when wielded by an experienced dominatrix.

Sissy Maid Camp

Have you ever fantasied about going to a camp where you would be trained to be a proper sissy maid? Do you wish a place existed where sissies are made to wear the highest of heels, a maid's dress, and makeup at all times with other sissies?

In 'Sissy Maid Camp', our protagonist finds out exactly how much his life can change over a summer. After a double dinner date with his wife and her friends from work, the couple learns about a camp where men are sent to be trained and taught how to be a proper sissy maid. Being a curious closeted sissy, he is intrigued by the camp and decides to try it out. While at camp, they are taught how to do their hair, makeup, and nails. Along with their new beauty regimen, they are trained to cook, clean, and serve their mistress diligently. A set of rules is instilled in the sissies, which requires them to stay quiet, curtsey, wear chastity, and act as girly as possible at all times. If a sissy disobeys or strays from the rules, they are punished swiftly. Although feminization surgery is not a requirement for camp, most of the sissies find themselves longing for a breast augmentation of their own. Over the course of the summer, our sissy learns that nothing will be the same when they return home from camp. They will continue to live as a sissy maid for their mistress permanently. Enjoy the tale as you witness the complete feminization of a young man into a sissy house maid eager to serve.

Cat And Mouse

Have you ever fantasied about becoming a personal sissy pet for a beautiful young woman?

In the story 'Cat and Mouse', we meet a young man named Bona who is down on his luck. After being unfairly accused of ratting on the mob family he works for, he comes within seconds of losing his life. When the mob boss's daughter steps in and asks to have Bona as her personal toy, Bona believes he has dodged a bullet. As he is stripped of his clothes, shaved, painted with makeup, and forced to wear a short latex dress and ballet heels, Bona begins to wonder if becoming Elaina's new pet is better than the other scenario that he escaped. After being fitted for his new collar, leash, and chastity cage, he is locked in a small dark room with Elaina's other sissy pet. Bona is teased and tormented by his new roommate as he is trained and feminized by his 19-year-old mistress. To cement his new role, Bona is given a full feminization surgery complete with a set of DD breasts and facial reconstructive surgery. He is humiliated and paraded in front of his old coworkers while completely feminized as a sissy pet. Will the sissy learn to accept their role and listen to what they're told, or will they try to fight and run away?

My Body Swap With Candi

Do you wish that you could shed your male body and experience lovemaking as a beautiful, sensual woman?

In 'My Body Swap with Candi', we follow a young man who is a frequent visitor at a local motel that prostitutes use as a meetup location. Having had many sessions with several ladies at the establishment, he has become well acquainted with everyone there except for one woman named Candi. While paying Candi a visit, he is surprised by her demeanor and unusual comments throughout their session. By the end, he is told that he has made a huge mistake and that he must pay for it. After running out and back to his home, he receives a call from a mysterious woman named Pixi. She informs him that because of his actions, he will inhabit the body of the woman he just slept with. However, while he inhabits the body for one week, he will be required to fulfill her duties or be stuck in the body forever. Thinking that the call is a joke, he dismisses the assertions made by Pixi and tells her where she can stick it. Before hanging up the phone, Pixi gives one last instruction. If he reaches an orgasm at any point during the week, he will live the rest of his life in Candi's body. After hanging up the phone, he slips into the deepest sleep of his life. Waking up the next morning, he thinks he is dreaming when he looks down at a set of his very own DD breasts. Running to the bathroom, he looks into the mirror and discovers that what Pixi said was true. Stuck in Candi's body with only one way out, he must fulfill Candi's responsibilities while being careful to not have a release. After meeting with his first few clients, he quickly discovers how sensitive his new body is and just how hard it will be to keep himself from orgasming. Does the young man have what it takes to keep his new body under control, or will he be stuck as Candi forever?

Paying Lip Service

Have you ever wondered what it would be like to become a real life sissy prostitute?

In the story 'Paying Lip Service', we witness the complete transformation of Billie Jean, the mattress king, to the BJ queen. After becoming indebted to a pimp in town with no way to pay him back, Billie is given a makeover and dressed as one of the prostitutes that works the streets. Knowing that they can't trust Billie to not run away, he is tied up and forced to pay lip service to the clients who visit them. Realizing how long it will take to pay off his debts, Billie asks if there is anything he can do to charge more and be finished sooner. The girls grant his request and have him brought in for a breast augmentation and lip fillers. Now further in debt, Billie will have to service even more clients before he has paid back what he owes. Billie's journey takes one twist after another as he is led down a path he may never return from. Will he ever be able to reclaim his old life or be stuck as the BJ queen forever?

Trained To Be A Sissy Pony

Have you ever fantasized about becoming a sissy pony? Do you wish that you could be dressed in a latex bodysuit, corset, pony boots, chastity cage, pony tail plug, and bit gag?

'Trained to be a Sissy Pony' puts you inside the heels of a man who is thrust into a part of the BDSM world he never knew existed. After being forcibly taken to a property where the owners are professional sissy pony trainers, he is given the full treatment and made to live as a full-time sissy pony. While dressed in a full body latex bodysuit, bone crushing under bust corset, heelless high heel boots that resemble pony legs, and hoof gloves, he is bound in a way that does not allow any mobility of his arms. He is completely helpless as he is forced to wear a chastity cage and a pony tail plug that dangles behind him. As he is trying to cope with the overwhelming nature of his new outfit, he is trained how to walk and act like a proper sissy pony should. His new owners groom him and paint him with makeup before presenting him to the whole world on a live video stream. Every part of his ego is torn to shreds, as he is forced to embody a sissy pony and start thinking of himself as such. Enjoy this steamy fantasy that puts you in the mind of a sissy pony who learns what it means to be ridden long and hard.

The Doll Designer

Have you ever wondered how it would feel to become a real life sissy doll? Does the thought of wearing a latex bodysuit and high heels excite you?

In 'The Doll Designer', we follow a young man who is getting to know a woman he just started dating. He can't help but feel inadequate, as this rich, beautiful woman would typically be out of his league. As he gets to know her, he finds out that she is a 'consultant' and lives in one of the wealthier neighborhoods in town. After one of their dates, she invites the young man back to her house to take their relationship to the next level. Once the young man steps into her house, he falls into a world he never knew existed. The naïve young man believes that if he goes along with what she is asking for long enough, they will eventually make love. As he is painted with makeup, dressed in high heels and lingerie, and bound, he starts to realize that she may have other plans for him. While tied up and unable to fight back, she marches him to her basement, where she uses sissy hypnosis to mold his brain to her desires. The sissy tries to fight back as she punishes him and uses everything in her power to break his will. But, once the sissy is stuffed into his latex doll bodysuit, escape will become near impossible. Will the sissy accept his role as a mindless sissy doll or try to fight back and break free at any opportunity that presents itself?

The Sissy Training Center

Have you ever dreamt of attending a sissy training center, where your only responsibility is to follow instructions and become an ideal, submissive sissy?

When a young man wakes up at 'The Sissy Training Center' with no memory of how he arrived, he quickly discovers that his captors have augmented his body in ways that he can never reverse. Looking down over himself, he finds that his chest has been sculpted with perky, round DD boobs. His silhouette has become a perfect hourglass figure while his face has been surgically enhanced to reflect the ideal feminine appearance. The only thing left that marks him as a man is now locked securely between his legs.

After being forcibly dressed in a latex catsuit and high heel booties, he is bound and gagged before being brought to the lower level of the facility, where he will be trained to become the perfect, submissive sissy. They train him with the S.I.S.S.Y. acronym and remind him daily that he is Submissive, he is Inferior, he is Sensitive, he is Silent, and he is always Yearning. Any deviation from the rules is recognized and dealt with swiftly through bondage related punishments. As a part of the training, the new sissy quickly realizes that it is not enough to allow the guards to have their way with him, but he must live out the sissy acronym and show that he yearns for their lovemaking. This trip through 'The Sissy Training Center' will keep the pages turning as you learn what brought the young man to this mysterious center and what he must do to find fulfillment inside of it.

The Sissy Slave Experience

In 'The Sissy Slave Experience', we follow a man in his mid-twenties who finds a service online that helps sissies explore their deepest desires. The service has a few options to choose from, where the sissy can explore their unique fantasies during a one-week immersive experience. After signing up for their program, he is required to come while dressed for the program. When he arrives at the address given to him, he is already dressed in a full-body latex catsuit, five inch high heel boots, and leather gloves while fully made up with his hair styled femininely. As a part of the required outfit, he must wear a chastity cage and plug. When he walks up to the front door to begin his experience, he realizes that he is either at the wrong address or that he may have been scammed. As he gets in his car and plans to leave, he is confronted by two men who take him to an unknown location. With a bag over his head, the two men bring the crossdresser into their basement and proceed to tie him up with a leather arm binder, a devious gag, ankle cuffs, and a collar with a leash attached. Although he had signed up for a one-week program similar to this, he fears that this experience may never come to an end. This hot and steamy story will leave you aching for more as it keeps you on the edge.